how to date a widow 101

John Polo

better not bitter widower

how to date a widow 101

John Polo of Better Not Bitter Widower

Copyright © 2019 by John Polo

All rights reserved. No part of this publication may be reproduced, distributed, or transmitted in any for or by any means, including photocopying, recording, or other electronic or mechanical methods, without the prior written permission of the publisher, except in the case of brief quotations embodied in critical reviews and certain other noncommercial used permitted by copyright law.

www.betternotbitterwidower.com

Graphic on page 39 courtesy of Freedesignfile.

Before you start reading, let me make a few statements about this book.

Those of you who have read my first two books have grown used to some pretty profound writing.

Yes, dude can write!

(Me, I'm dude)

You're also use to some weird ass humor.

In truth, this book is none of that.

This book isn't meant to move your heart, or touch your soul.

This book isn't meant to make you laugh, or cry.

This book is meant to serve as a quick "how to".

An actual guide for those who have met a widow (or widower) - who they are interested in.

This book is meant to help guide them on how to date, and potentially love, a widowed person.

And yes, it is also meant for you: **the widowed person.**

To serve as a guide for what you might expect.

A guide to help you see the type of love, that you are worthy of.

I hope it helps

When I was 22, my mom wanted to introduce me to a widow.

I told her "I will never date a widow."

My sister was standing there, and in a taken aback tone, asked me "Why not?"

"I'm not competing with a dead man. Fuck that."

Oh, *how I've grown*

So you met a widow, huh?

You haven't run yet?

Good deal.

Do you like her?

Let me ask that question again, but in a different way…..

Do you like her, *like her?*

As in, is she worth the effort?

If your answer is "yes".

Then let's begin....

"Don't just accept the fact she will always love her husband –
but LOVE the fact that she will always love her husband.

For his love & his loss – have BOTH helped shape the woman –
that you so claim to love, today."

the basics:

1) her husband is dead

2) so if you are jealous

3) You are jealous of a dead man

just sayin'

"He said, 'well if he gets a shrine at your house, I do, too.' No, actually, after a month of dating, you certainly do not!"

Jenny

"He told me that it appeared I still loved my husband because I would post about him on social media. Sure do! He was such a douche canoe."

Whitney

Jayne

"He asked me when I was going to get over my dead husband. It was our first date. I was taken aback. I could not believe that those words came out of his mouth."

"What did you say?" I asked in response.

"I told him I would never get over my husband.

I then told him that I would be moving forward with my life.

But certainly not with him."

Jayne, one of my coaching clients, then proceeded to grab her coat and immediately left the date.

"How did it make you feel when you said that and left?" I asked.

"Amazing. And empowered," she responded.

Tell her that she can't speak of her lost love.

Or, don't tell her that, but pout every time she mentions his name.

She might stay with you.

But she's sure not going to respect you.

Resentment will build.

Do you really want to make her feel bad for her pain?

& for her grief?

Or do you want her to adore you ….

For your love & for your support

The more you support her

The more you embrace not
only her heartache

But her strength, her bravery
and her resiliency

The more you honor
the love and the loss

The more she will value you

The choice is yours

4 the widow:

Listen, the truth is, dating a widow isn't the easiest thing in the world.

You are not perfect.

The person you are dating is not going to be perfect.

& if we are going to be completely honest here for a second – your spouse wasn't perfect, **either.**

Michelle and I had an amazing marriage

Amazing

But for various reasons that I won't get into here -
she wasn't always the best at showing love

She was an amazing wife

But not very good at communication,
or expressing her thoughts and emotions

So when she did - it was amazing

Nobody is perfect

I'm not

She wasn't

It's not about finding someone perfect

It's about finding someone who you adore

Flaws, shortcomings ~ *and all*

"He doesn't always get it, he doesn't always understand, but he tries. He always tries. I couldn't ask for anything more than that."

Briann

4 the widow:

Do you have the ability to read minds?

No?

Well, your new love interest probably doesn't either.

Furthermore, as we are grieving & healing, there are many times when we don't exactly know what we need for ourselves.

So, **how in the world** are they supposed to know?

IF YOU WANT A TRULY HEALTHY RELATIONSHIP, COMMUNICATION IS KEY.

Tell them what comforts you, and what doesn't.

Tell them what you are feeling, and thinking.

Allow them to know what you want, and need.

So that you can then see, if they have the ability to love you ~ the way that you want, *and need.*

More basics:

- She is always going to love her husband

- The statement above is **ABSOLUTELY** no reflection of her feelings towards you

- Often times, falling in love again brings with it a tremendous amount of guilt and fear. The fact that she is willing to open her heart again is **brave AF.**

- When our spouse passes away, a part of us goes with them. We are, in effect, like a stranger to ourselves. We have to rebuild. Yes, you're getting to know her, but keep in mind – she's likely also getting to know herself – *as well*.

There is no actual finish line

Grief never ends

Not after a truly profound loss

It changes

& it evolves

Absolutely

It continues to look different overtime

But no, *it never full goes away*

If you are going to try to date her, and eventually, love her ~ it is **VITALLY** important that you understand how she can be both happy and sad – all at once

Please do not ever think to yourself, "Well I should be enough to make her happy"

- Her husband died

- She has been through **HELL**

The pain from such a loss does not simply "go away"

There will be times when she is happy

There will be times when she is sad

There will be times when she is *both, happy and sad*

Example

My wife and I got married at a courthouse, 4 days after her diagnosis.

5 days before her first surgery was scheduled to take place.

She was violently ill, couldn't stop throwing up & was in extreme pain.

Immediately after the wedding, we headed to the ER
where we would stay for 5 days until her first surgery.

After the cancer came roaring back and she was pronounced terminal,
we decided to plan a real wedding.

She died 2 weeks before our ceremony was scheduled to take place.

I had dreamt of watching her walk down the aisle since I was 17 years old.

And I never got to.

Now

Imagine I fall in love again.

Imagine I have a real wedding one day.

Imagine I am watching my beautiful bride walk down the aisle.

This new woman, *who I have fallen in love with*.

Do you think I will be happy?

HELL YEAH, I will be happy.

Do you think that part of me will be sad?

Knowing that I never got to watch Michelle walk down that aisle?

YES, part of me will be sad – *as well*.

This is one example of how we can be both happy and sad.

This is one example of how grief, never fully ends.

Get it?

Got it?

Cool

Listen to me, I am very smart *(about certain things)*:

- Communication is VERY important. In a whole bunch of different ways. But for the purposes of this page, let's focus on you responding to texts and such. PTSD amongst widowed people is a very real thing. Many widowed people lost their loves suddenly. Sometimes situations involved trying desperately to get in contact with them for hours, or even days. If you truly want to date a widow, it is really important that you understand this. It is really important that you not go AWOL on her. Please, *do your very best to make sure that she does not have to worry that you are dead.*

- Please reread the statement above

- If you can't appreciate and understand the importance of what I just said, **you probably are not ready to date a widowed person.**

If you're feeling overwhelmed by the content of this book,
I would encourage you to take a short break, and then keep reading.

She's worth it.

Widowed people's self-esteem and self-worth tend to plummet. This isn't always the case, but for many of us this is true. There are actual reasons for this. While I certainly don't want her relying solely on you for her self-esteem and/or self-worth, please know that you do have the ability to help her in these areas.

- Tell her what she means to you
- And how she brightens your every day
- Remind her of her inner beauty
- And her worth
- Tell her that you adore her

I mean after all, she's just **so damn** *adorable.*

If you're a widowed person reading this and thinking to yourself, "But who is going to want me (insert all of the negative things you tell yourself about yourself) ...."

we REALLY need to work on that.

The way that we see ourselves **IS EVERYTHING.**

Guys: IT IS EVERYTHING.

Fill your own damn shoes

This is an analogy I use with my clients. It's much better when spoken, but since I really want to include it in this book – here it is in written form:

My wife's shoes are in the corner.

They are her shoes.

Just sittin' there.

DO NOT TOUCH THEM.

She was 1 in 7 billion.

Just as I am.

Just as you are.

I don't want another Michelle, *because there will never be another Michelle.*

What I want in any new love interest, is what I also want in myself.

To be the best version of themselves - **that they** can possibly be.

In other words, *fill your own damn shoes!*

No joke: **go back** and read that previous page again

If you can master that concept, you'll be golden

after everything she has been through……

SHE NEEDS A MAN

NOT A BOY.

Let's talk about not so great marriages

I was at a conference once and one of the attendees said the following:

"Only those who had good, or great marriages, truly know grief."

THAT IS 100 MILLION PERCENT FALSE.

Those who had difficult, or even bad to horrible marriages, also know grief.

For many of them, they experience complicated grief.

& complicated grief is AN UGLY ASS BEAST.

PLEASE, PLEASE, PLEASE
if the widowed person you are dating
had a difficult or bad/horrible marriage, please
DO NOT EVER minimize their pain.

Their pain, if I am being completely honest, has layers to it that is usually not seen in those of us who had good, or great marriages.

Saying something like, "Well he was horrible to you anyways so I don't understand what the problem is" is quite possibly one of the worst things that could come out of your mouth.

- Do not minimize their pain

- Do not minimize their pain

- **Do not minimize their pain**

the people who come into your life now ~ are not responsible for the damage done, by the people of your past

john polo coaching.

"Kevin is always so amazing about my grief. He is patient, and understanding. He is respectful, and accepts that I will always have a place for Clarence in my heart. That being said, he also knows what Clarence did to me. He knows how he hurt me, and how it impacts me still to this day. There's a part of me that thinks Kevin might hate Clarence because of that, but what I admire most about this man, is that he never puts those emotions on me. He just listens to me, and loves me the way I know that I deserve to be loved."

Kelly

Lean into who you are

Clients will often tell me that they don't think they will be able to meet someone because they are "so awkward".

If you're awkward, **be awkward!**

Do you know what I miss about Michelle the most?

Other than absolutely everything.

Her bumping into walls.

Yup.

I miss her dorkiness.

Her weirdness.

Her unique ways.

That's what made me truly fall in love with her.

& she loved my odd ass just the same!

Be who you are

The right person will adore you; *for you*

Your weird ass self

I often hear people say "I will only date another widowed person, because they are the only ones who can truly understand".

Look, **I get that thought pattern.**

Do I personally prefer to date a widow?

Actually, if I'm being honest – *yes, I do.*

That being said, I am certainly not going to limit myself to only dating someone who has lost a spouse.

I have many clients, and friends, who have fallen in love again with non-widowed individuals.

Non-widowed individuals who are loving and supportive.

Non-widowed individuals who they have built beautiful lives with.

If we're going to open our hearts again, let us also open our minds a bit – *as well.*

a page for notes

Self-sabotage

If I could only work on one topic with clients for the rest of my career, it would be this.

Self-sabotage.

This world can be hard enough to live in, without us continuously getting in **our own damn way.**

As I see it, there are 4 main reasons why people self-sabotage:

- Low self-esteem

- Poor self-worth (this is the most dangerous of all)

- Guilt and Fear

Other, less important/dangerous, but still very real reasons why we self-sabotage:

- Stubbornness, ego, insecurities, fear of judgment, spite

I have seen first-hand the unbelievable impact that self-sabotage can have on a person's life.

Guys, we literally have the ability to

destroy our own lives.

For any of those reasons I listed, but especially because of low *self-worth*.

Regardless of What They Say

My wife had a horrible life.

Horrible.

The stories she would tell me.

The people who abused her.

And abandoned her.

The things that she endured.

When we dated in High School she would cry to me.

"Everyone hurts or leaves me John. And you will too."

I wouldn't have.

But it didn't matter.

With self-worth so destroyed.

She sabotaged the relationship.

Allowing her past pain.

To affect her present decisions.

She impacted her future.

In profoundly horrible ways.

I have always known the value of self-worth.

So much more important than that of self-esteem.

It impacts our present. And our future.

But more importantly.

It impacts our soul.

Those who have programmed us to believe that we are not worthy.

Worthy of love.

And respect.

Worthy of being treated the right way.

Their behavior a direct result of who THEY are.

And not of who YOU are.

Yet their behavior only changing you.

In a negative way.

Never them.

Their inability to grow.

Creating the deep inner desire for them to destroy.

Your ability to grow.

"You didn't lie John,"

Michelle said to me as we held hands in her hospice bed a few days before her last breath.

"What do you mean?"

I asked.

"You told me that you would never leave.

And you didn't lie."

◇◇◇◇◇◇◇◇◇◇◇◇◇◇◇◇◇◇◇◇◇◇◇◇◇◇◇◇◇◇◇◇◇◇◇◇◇◇◇

Go where the love is.

You deserve it.

Regardless of what they say.

This is a message I sent to a client, who had met her Prince Charming.

But was too scared to go all in.

She was so scared that he might die.

As her husband did.

She was so scared of this, that she refused to fully give her heart.

To the man who had stolen her heart.

She had what she wanted, right in front of her.

But her fear wouldn't allow her to go for it.

She was literally about to lose, exactly what it was ~ that she feared, she might one day lose.

> Seems to me like maybe it's time to go all in. Cause you're smiling. Cause he makes you smile. And cause you deserve a life ~ with more smiles

I know I already said this on page 22 but I feel the need to repeat it right here.

HER OPENING HER HEART UP AGAIN TO LOVE IS **BRAVE AF.**

So, I'm going to need you to be brave too – ok?

"On more than one occasion he would tell me that he knew he was my consolation prize. The truth is that's not how I looked at him at all. Needless to say, it didn't work out."

Ilise

not brave homie!

Not brave at all

When do I tell them I am a widow?

About a year after Michelle passed, I was talking to someone who asked if I was ready to start dating.

I told them that I thought that I was.

They suggested to me that I not tell anyone I was a widower until the 3rd date.

How. Da. Fuck. Do. You. Go. On. A. Date. And. Not. Mention. The. Fact. That.

You. Have. A. Dead. Wife.

Like, *I don't even understand* how that would work?

Look: if you're just looking to go out and get you some booty, then fine – tell them or not, it's your choice.

But, if you're looking for **absolutely anything** more than that – then there really is no reason to tiptoe around this.

If someone is too weak to deal with the fact that you are a widowed person on date 1 ....

they are going to be too weak to deal with the fact that you are a widowed person on date 24, *as well.*

Let's go back to that last sentence for a moment.

For the sake of clarity, just because someone doesn't want to date a widowed person ~ doesn't make them a bad person.

I have always been a good guy to my core.

But that 22-year-old kid who said "I don't want to complete with a dead man. Fuck that.", he just didn't have the maturity level that it takes.

I was too insecure.

I wasn't a bad guy.

It just wasn't for me.

Had I met and started dating a widow, it definitely would not have worked out.

Let's talk about: **children**

How in the world am I going to write a brief page about this? ?

Let me just say the following:

Creating a bond/eventually loving a child you did not create, is **SUCH beautiful thing.**

Truly.

Please keep the following in mind:
- Her kids come first
- They are grieving too
- It may take time for them to warm up to you, or – *they may become attached to you VERY quickly*
- Try not to let either of the above possibilities scare you off
- They are likely to be confused by the whole situation. As are you. As is she.
- The difference is you guys are adults. *And they are not.*
- If you and her are going to get serious, and you are going to be a part of her children's lives, **y'all better communicate REALLY well throughout the process.**
- About what is expected. And what is not.
- If you think dating a widow comes with a learning curve, becoming a part of her children's lives comes with an even steeper learning curve.
- If you think dating a widow can be a beautiful thing, because of their heart, bravery and amount of love that they have to give ~ wait until you see how beautiful building a relationship with her children can be.

"These two.

I think he loves her almost as much as he loves me.

And she feels the same way."

Kelly

how to date a widow 101

"When I see Charley interact, accept and love another man in her life, it makes me happy. Watching her with my new love, it touches my heart in a way that I didn't know was possible. On occasion, something funny will happen though. While watching them together, all of a sudden, a rush of sadness will overcome me. As amazing as it is, sometimes the reality hits that this isn't the way it was supposed to be. Charley is supposed to be playing with Chad. He is supposed to be here, but he's not."

Krystal

This is normal. Please do not take it personally.

Even as she adores the way that you adore her child, the sadness is likely to make an occasional appearance.

Please be confident enough in who you are, and in what you bring to the table, to not let it make you think that you are not worthy.

Or less than.

Be strong.

For her.

For you.

& for them

Random Ramblings from a Rambling Man

- Skin hunger is a **VERY** real thing

- **We move forward.** Not on.

- We can move forward as we grieve
  & we can grieve as we move forward

What do I do on

His Birthday: **love and support her**

Their Anniversary: **love and support her**

The Day He Died: **love and support her**

An average Tuesday: **love and support her**

Will she ever love me as much as she loved him?

DO NOT **EVER** ASK HER THIS QUESTION.

& honestly – don't even ask yourself that question

It's a horrible question

In the case of a widowed person, the heart is large enough for 2...

how to date a widow 101

Meet Jessica

Jessica met the first man she would ever love, Michael, in Spanish class.

He was 14.

She, one year younger.

"A mutual friend introduced the two of us and I just ignored him. I guess he didn't like that because he pulled a prank on me and I ended up slapping him across the face.

Believe it or not, from that point on, we were best friends."

One night as the two were driving, a song came on the radio.

"Back at One" by Brian McKnight.

As Jessica tells it, Michael pulled the car over and asked her to get out.

It was raining but, reluctantly, and with a little nudge from her best bud, she did.

"He turned up the radio and he made me dance in the middle of the street with him. In the rain. It was at that very moment that we fell in love."

The two dated for a number of years and married in 2003.

Michael and Jessica spent ten years together as man and wife.

They loved each other. And the life that they had built.

On February 6, 2013, after complications from a routine surgery, Michael unexpectedly fell into a coma.

For the next eight days, Jessica laid by her husband's side.

And she refused to leave.

"On the day he died, I climbed into bed with him and I wrapped his arms around me.

And I placed my head on his chest."

On February 14, 2013, Michael took his last breath in the physical form.

"He died, but I felt like I did, too. We all did. He was our everything."

Before he got sick, Michael had made Jessica promise to take him to a concert.

"Although not wanting to, I ended up going to that concert. And that is where I met Kyle. I met him at the concert I was supposed to go to with Michael. To this day, that very fact still floors me," Jessica recalled.

Nearly five years after the passing of her first love, Kyle and Jessica became man and wife on December 26, 2017.

"It's so weird loving two people. The way I love Michael, I am proud of being a wife again. It is amazing to still feel that love for Michael and still be able to love another so deeply.

Michael wasn't my first chapter, and Kyle isn't my second chapter.

Each man is their own separate book.

I realized, on this journey, that my heart is capable of loving two.

I never would have thought it was possible.

But **my heart is capable of loving two."**

"I don't care if the love I have for my wife makes all new potential love interests run away. Any woman who doesn't understand a heart large enough for two, lacks the depth that I require."

Me

Sexy Time

Be patient with her when it comes to intimacy.
There could be times that she gets "upset" for no reason.
This isn't a reflection of you, nor your sexiness **(insert eye roll)**.

A Step Further:

Yes, intimacy means in the bedroom, *but is also means so much more.*

She may actually be fine with a sexual act, but have a hard time holding hands, or cuddling.

If she does get upset, she is likely to **BE UPSET.**

Be a calming presence for her.

Do not make her feel sadder, guiltier or more confused *than she already feels.*

"Sometimes we don't want you to try to figure out what the right thing is to say, sometimes we just need you to hold us.

In silence."

Ashley

Fb status & wedding ring

- While it may not make sense to you, for many of us Facebook often feels like one of the last ways we are connected to our deceased love. While the truth is we can carry their love and memory with us every single day, in our hearts it can feel as though changing our relationship status on Facebook is severing one of our last ties to them. Please – **allow her to do this in her own time.** Don't pressure, or force it upon her.

- Additionally, please don't pressure her to mark that the two of you are in a relationship on Facebook. I'm not saying you should wait 34 years before doing this, but it's really important you give her the grace to do this in her own time. Not only can it be really difficult emotionally, but we also have to take into account that she may be worried about the reaction of the outside world.

- She'll take off her ring, or move it to another finger, when she is good and ready. *Chillax.*

Just so we're clear:

Not dating again is perfectly fine TOO

Just as dating doesn't mean you're over it

Not dating, **doesn't mean you're stuck**

Honestly, after the Hell that you have endured, the key is to

EMPOWER yourself enough to live however it is that YOU WANT TO LIVE!

"I don't know how to be a girlfriend. I know how to be a wife".

Eva

4 the widow:

If you don't know how to be a girlfriend, chances are he doesn't exactly know how to be a boyfriend to a widow.

Think about it.

As long as he is kind, loving and willing to learn – *have a little patience.*

As widowed people, we can't expect complete patience and total understanding from the person we are dating while having a 100% no tolerance level for their own internal growth.

"My boyfriend was amazing. I mean truly, unbelievably amazing. He was so supportive of my grief and my love for my late husband. Until one day, when he got frustrated with me. We were with a group of friends on vacation and I had a breakdown. This was about a year into our relationship. In a super annoyed tone, he asked me if it was always going to be this way. We got into a huge fight. Looking back though, I now realize he is only human, and that seeing me hurt, hurt him as well. We have now been together for over two years, and to this day that was the only day that he ever showed frustration. He isn't perfect, but neither am I."

Josi

We talked a little about children, but the focus of those pages was on younger children.

So for a moment, let's talk about adult children.

I have to tell you guys something:

I have 60-year-old clients who start dating again and their 40-year-old, adult children, throw a complete shit fit.

There's a lot I could say to this, but it's a very complicated situation and this book is meant as more of an overview.

So let me just say this:

If her children are giving her a hard time, you adding to it by making her feel guilty over their behavior is not the right approach.

It's not going to help her, you – or the situation.

Same with her friends.

Some of her friends might not be supportive.

This is NOT her fault.

So please don't make it her fault.

Be her teammate.

Not her opponent.

4 the widow:

I personally don't care if you date 3 months after your spouse passes away, 3 years after your spouse passes away, *or if you never date ever again.*

I don't care.

I just want you to be as happy, peaceful and healthy as you can possibly be.

I am all for you taking your time. Working on yourself. Discovering the "new you".

I am all for you finding some version of happiness, outside of a romantic relationship.

Yes. Absolutely.

Those are **VERY** good things.

That being said, if you are a widowed person who wants to date again but has it stuck in your mind that you need to reach some inner level of perfection before you can put yourself back out there, I just want to say:

We can walk and chew gum at the same time.

It's probably NOT a good idea to tell her you don't think she's ready to date just because you can't wrap your mind around the timeline she is on.

Every person is different.

I know people who had absolutely amazing marriages who date 3 months out. And I know people who had absolutely amazing marriages who never date ever again.

I know people who had horrible marriages who date 3 months out. And I know people who had absolutely horrible marriages who never date ever again.

If you don't feel comfortable with the timeline she is on, *that's on you.*

Not her.

Get ready for it ▪ ▪ ▪ ▪

Sit Down. And Shut Up.

Sit down.

And shut up.

Serious question: Is your spouse six feet under?
Oh, wait, are they a pile of ashes?

No?

They aren't?

Wow.

Okay.

Cool.

Then, sit down.

And shut up.

My wife's name was Michelle. She's gone.

Once a widow. Always a widow.

Once a widower. Always a widower.

Sit down.

And shut up.

Unless you watched your spouse die. Unless you buried your spouse.
Unless you burned your spouse.

Sit down.

And shut up.

Do not tell a widow or widower how they should be living.

Do not tell a widow or widower how they should be acting.

And, please – for the love of all that is right in this world, PLEASE – do NOT tell a widow or widower when they should try to love again.

I am sick of seeing widows and widowers vilified for trying to pick up the pieces of their lives.

I am sick of seeing widows and widowers vilified for trying to find companionship again. For trying to find love again.

Hell, for trying to find ANYTHING again!

We are lost souls. On a journey to find our self again.

And YOU want to judge?

You?

Do you know the courage it takes to go back out there after your spouse has died?

After you watched them die of cancer.
Or a massive heart attack. Or suicide.

After you watched them fall to 60 pounds.
Having bowel movements on themselves. Having horrific hallucinations so bad that seeing them like that strangled your soul.

After you watched them fall to their knees. And clutch their chest. And take their last breath.

After you walked in on their body. Dead. Because they took their own life.

You have no idea.

Do you have any idea how badly the loss of a spouse messes with your mind? With your heart? With your soul?

No. You don't.

So, sit down.

And shut up.

You are not allowed to judge.

how to date a widow 101

You are not allowed to pass judgment as you drive home to your spouse.

You are not allowed to pass judgment as you eat dinner with your spouse.

You are not allowed to pass judgment as you cuddle up on the couch with your spouse.

You are not allowed to pass judgment as you have sexy time with your spouse.

You. Are. Not. Allowed. To. Pass. Judgment.

Sit down.

And shut up.

Stop judging.

Stop thinking that you know what the Hell you are talking about.

Because you do not.

Your life wasn't ripped from you.

Your future wasn't destroyed.

Sit down.

And shut up.

This was not our choice.

This was not a breakup. Stop comparing.

This was not a divorce. Stop comparing.

This was not the loss of a grandpa. Stop comparing.

This was not the loss of Uncle Thomas. Stop comparing.

And, for Heaven's sake, this was NOT the loss of your damn CAT. Stop comparing!

This was the loss of a soulmate.

Our love.

Our other half.

Our life.

Our future.

Sit down.

And shut up.

The next time you see a widow or widower try to pick themselves up, dust themselves off and "get back out there."

You have 2 choices.

You can either sit down and shut up.

Or:

You can give them a standing ovation.

For their heart. For their courage. For their bravery.

Those are your two options.

And your ONLY two options.

Because. You. Do. Not. Know.

Rant. Over.

4 the widow:

If I'm being honest, one of the other things that
I see on a regular basis is y'all chasing assholes.

& then as soon as the good guy comes into your life,
you take him for granted.

To the point where some of you are even mean to him.

Some of you guys didn't realize this book would be a **reality check**
for you too, *did ya?*

Look, if you've met a great guy who wants nothing more than to treat you
the right way – either value him, or let him go.

He doesn't deserve to be treated like crap, *either.*

& for you …..

Just because she's a widow, it doesn't mean she's always right

You can be kind, loving and supportive – *without being a pushover*

- Allowing her to walk all over you is a sure-fire way to lose her respect

By the way, if you chase assholes – there are reasons why you do this.

Reasons that don't meet the eye.

I'm not going to get into that here because that is an entire book in itself.

The person we choose to be with is, as you know, one of the most important decisions we will make in our life.

If you keep choosing the wrong men, I believe I can help you to break out of that cycle.

Sign up for **my coaching,** and let's get to work.

> I need to share something just to get it off my chest. Let me preface that there is no pressure from the guy I started seeing for sex. I want to have sex with him but since becoming a widow, I actually struggle with having sex with a guy I want to date long term. One night stand? No problem. FWB? It is on! You want to get to know me and date me? Ummm, let me become a nun. I am trying to figure out why I am this way.

I know why she is this way ….

Do you?

Hi,
I just want to say youre never even going to allow yourself the chance of meeting Price Charming
~ if you keep wasting your time on that douche bag

Have a nice day.
john polo coaching.

He said to Me:

"I don't always understand your anxiety, but I'll lie down next to you whenever you need to lie down, and for as long as you need to."

Lisa

"You'll never have to spend this day alone again if you don't want to, as long as I'm living. I know how much you love him and how upsetting today is for you."

Olivia

"You are just so damn brave."

Brooke

You deserve to be loved,

the way that you deserve to be loved

Every person is different.

So I am not going to tell you what to say, or not to say.

Generally speaking though, widowed people aren't crazy about platitudes.

"Everything happens for a reason" or "Time heals all" usually just annoys the shit out of us.

"I don't always know the best thing to say, but I am always here for you," is a much better way to approach someone during a moment of great pain.

Like all humans, widowed people have insecurities.

Sometimes, these insecurities run deep.

If she needs reassurance: **reassure her!**

Her asking for your reassurance shouldn't be annoying.

It is actually a testament to how much she wants to be with you.

If she didn't care about you, she wouldn't need reassurance.

Once she feels comfortable, and trusts you are not going anywhere, **she will probably need less.**

:: That doesn't mean you should give her less, but the need may subside ::

do **NOT** do these things

Ask her to take pictures down

She will take down whatever it is that she decides to take down - WHEN SHE IS READY.

Ask her to get rid of his clothes

She will do whatever it is that she decides to do with his clothes – WHEN SHE IS READY

Imply that her pain is not valid because they were not married

Or because their time together was short

A page from my 1st book

Last night I went out with a group of local widowed people.
Some I knew, some I didn't.

Towards the end of the night a conversation began
with one of the widows I had never met before.

Michelle came up, so I explained some of the back story.

After we discussed Michelle, this woman made a comment
that had me a little confused.

Was she a widow?

Or perhaps just a friend of someone who decided
to tag along for the evening?

"Wait, are you a widow?" I asked.

She responded back with hesitation, telling me that she didn't know how
to respond to that because they were only engaged - and not married.

"You're a widow. You're a widow," I started.

"Well, I mean unless you don't want to be a widow.
You can call yourself whatever you want," I backed off a bit,
realizing that she may not want to be referred to as a widow.

"I personally think you are a widow though.
A piece of paper does not measure love," I concluded.

She hesitated, without response for a moment,
as she gave me a look of appreciation.

It was as if I was validating her pain, in a world that sometimes may not.

Let me be clear:

Never treat someone else's pain as less than yours simply because they
do not have a marriage license.

Those who didn't make it official in time deserve
all of the same love and support as the rest of us.

#piece #of #paper #or #not

Idealistic

Let me take a second to say something here.

I know that some might be reading this and thinking to themselves that it's a bunch of bullshit.

Some may feel that I am taking an approach that is way too idealistic.

If you feel that way, I urge you to go back and reread page 18.

To the person dating a widow:

No, I do not expect you to be perfect. Nor do I expect you to be the most loving person in the history of the world. BUT, if this book can give you even one helpful tip on how to best love and support her, then I feel like my job here is done. And if you feel like I am raising the bar too high, **perhaps your bar – is too low.**

To the widow:

You need to go back and reread page 18 as well. I was not the perfect husband. And my wife was not the perfect wife. You were not the perfect partner. And neither was your deceased love. Sometimes I see people settling. And sometimes I see people ruining amazing relationships because they are in pursuit of something that they did not even have with their late spouse: Perfection.

Please do not put this book down and think to yourself that you need to end it with an amazing person simply because he did not throw a parade for you on what would have been your 25th wedding anniversary.

That is **NOT** the purpose of this book.

Hi,

If she has a memorial tattoo, or wants to get one, and you don't like it.

You are probably not ready to date a widow.

We don't just miss them.

And the past.

We also miss, *the future missed.*

Please understand that this is not a reflection of you.

She could be over the moon happy about her life with you.

And still miss him.

She could be over the moon happy about her future with you.

And still miss, the future ~ ***that they missed.***

Kelly Hobbs Daniel
20 mins

I normally post these things in my widow groups because they already get it. But, well, they already get it. This is my real life.

I love Kevin with all my heart. When I say he has changed our lives, I'm not exaggerating. I have been happier and had more amazing days than I thought was ever going to be possible again in the last two months. But I also miss Clarence hard today. I looked at a picture of his brother this morning and saw Clarence's eyes looking back at me and it was all too much.

Being widowed and falling in love again is the scariest, most exciting, most confusing thing that I've ever faced. I'm sad because I miss Clarence. I'm elated because I have Kevin. I feel guilty for being sad. Then I feel guilty for being happy. It doesn't matter how much I know neither one of them wants me to feel this way. Grief comes when it comes. So does love. So I'm just going to put Clarence's wedding ring on, curl up with Kevin's pillow, and cry until I fall asleep or feel better.

#whatmygrieflookstoday

Her life being better with you than it was with him, in any way, shape or form – **is likely to fuck with her mind.**

A lot.

Love is Not a FB Meme

People have pain, and fear

People have guilt, and walls

People have scars

Communicate

Be loving

& kind

Be clear

About what you need

& don't need

The right person isn't going to know all of you

The right person is going to ....

Want to get to know all of you

Know what you deserve

Communicate what you expect

Understand that beautiful relationships are not stumbled upon

But built

& do not settle

#ever

fellas:
Make a conscious effort to look at her the way you looked at her Before she was yours

& watch how fast the relationship changes
john polo coaching.

Dear Ed,

For many years, I was happy to call you and Dawne my friends. I cherished the opportunities we had to spend together. We shared so many laughs, and so many bonding experiences over the great music that we all loved.

As you were getting ready to leave this world, Dawne would give me regular updates on your condition. My heart was breaking for her, and of course, for you.

After your passing, the friendship between Dawne and I began to drift a bit. That is until this past winter when I decided to pay her a visit as I was passing by the home that the two of you shared. After spending some time with her, I made a vow in my heart to be a much better friend, and so we remained in regular contact.

As our friendship continued to evolve, I began to notice things about her that I am sure you noticed as well.

I noticed how kind she was, and how beautiful.

I noticed her warmth, and the size of her heart.

Ed, it got to a point where every time she would smile, *I would melt.*

I went into this relationship knowing that you would always be an important part of it. And I wouldn't have it any other way. Dawne never makes me feel second best. She gives me the same level of commitment that she gave to you. I think because she has loved and lost before, she realizes how precious life is, and therefore takes none of this for granted.

There have been times when Dawne has gotten upset. Times when I was convinced my presence in her life was causing her much pain and anxiety. Moments of anger and despair broke my heart, because I could see how much they were breaking hers.

We worked on it together, and began to realize how fear, guilt and grief were impacting her ability to move forward. I can't imagine how scary this is for her. She is so brave.

Ed, I wanted to write you this letter today to say *Thank You*.

Thank you for being such a great friend to me.

Thank you for being such a GREAT husband to Dawne.

Thank you for bringing us together.

I know you had a hand in it.

And most importantly: Thank You for being you.

You were such an amazing soul.

I hope that I am making you proud my friend.

I love you. Good luck on your new adventure, until I see you again.

Jonathan H.

2 broken people coming together can be a beautiful thing …..

if they are not only willing to work on themselves,
but also willing - *to root on the other.*

Amanda Flanagan-Hoffman

Sunday at 11:34 PM

When your new husband comes home with flowers for a wedding anniversary that isn't even his... because he's not here to give them to me anymore... not to mention in my late husband & i's favorite colors.

8.18.12. 🤍

#IHaveTheBestHusbands

Love her the right way

She deserves it.

How to follow, or work with, John:

For access to my social media pages, books, journals, 1-on-1 coaching, courses, groups, events and more check out my website

@ www.betternotbitterwidower.com

"He is absolutely the best at what he does." – Anita

Having to date again after you thought you had found your forever really sucks. But, for those of us who want to find love again:

it only takes 1

Made in the USA
Monee, IL
01 August 2021